Major US Historical Wars

Native American Wars on the Western Frontier, 1866-1890

Leslie Galliker

 Mason Crest
Philadelphia

Mason Crest
450 Parkway Drive, Suite D
Broomall, PA 19008
www.masoncrest.com

Printed and bound in the United States of America.

CPSIA Compliance Information: Batch #MUW2015. For further information, contact Mason Crest at 1-866-MCP-Book.

3 5 7 9 8 6 4 2

Library of Congress Cataloging-in-Publication Data

ISBN: 978-1-4222-3357-3 (hc)
ISBN: 978-1-4222-8597-8 (ebook)

Major US Historical Wars series ISBN: 978-1-4222-3352-8

About the Author: Leslie Galliker lives in Jackson, New Jersey. She is a former reporter and medical transcriptionist. Leslie has three adult children and five grandchildren.

Picture Credits: Colorado Historical Society: 35; Denver Public Library: 31, 38, 41, 43, 44 (top), 50; Everett Historical: 48, 51; Independence National Historical Park, Philadelphia: 11; Library of Congress: 8, 19, 21, 22, 24, 25, 29 (left), 30, 32, 33, 36, 37, 42, 44 (bottom), 52, 53, 54; Little Bighorn Battlefield National Monument/National Park Service: 1; courtesy Museum of New Mexico, neg. no. 45968: 29 (right); National Archives: 14, 16, 17, 45, 47; used under license from Shutterstock, Inc.: 7, 15, 23, 40; Don Stivers Publishing: 29; The Woolaroc Museum: 12; U.S. Military Academy at West Point: 9; reproduced from *A Pictographic History of the Oglala Sioux*, by Amos Bad Heart Bull, text by Helen H. Blish, by permission of the University of Nebraska Press: 49.

Table of Contents

Introduction   5

Chapter 1: The Causes of Wars on the Frontier   7

Chapter 2: Reservation Life   19

Chapter 3: Warfare in the Southwest   27

Chapter 4: Warfare on the Plains
           during the 1860s   35

Chapter 5: Warfare on the Plains, 1874-1890   47

Chronology   56

Further Reading   60

Internet Resources   61

Index   62

Series Glossary   64

KEY ICONS TO LOOK FOR:

Words to Understand: These words with their easy-to-understand definitions will increase the reader's understanding of the text, while building vocabulary skills.

Sidebars: This boxed material within the main text allows readers to build knowledge, gain insights, explore possibilities, and broaden their perspectives by weaving together additional information to provide realistic and holistic perspectives.

Research Projects: Readers are pointed toward areas of further inquiry connected to each chapter. Suggestions are provided for projects that encourage deeper research and analysis.

Text-Dependent Questions: These questions send the reader back to the text for more careful attention to the evidence presented there.

Series Glossary of Key Terms: This back-of-the book glossary contains terminology used throughout this series. Words found here increase the reader's ability to read and comprehend higher-level books and articles in this field.

Other Titles in This Series

The American Revolution

The Civil War

The Cold War

The Korean War

Native American Wars on the Western Frontier (1866-1890)

US-Led Wars in Iraq, 1991-Present

The Vietnam War

War in Afghanistan: Overthrow of the Taliban and Aftermath

The War of 1812

World War I

World War II

Introduction

By Series Consultant Lt. Col. Jason R. Musteen

Lt. Col. Jason R. Musteen is a U.S. Army Cavalry officer and combat veteran who has held various command and staff jobs in Infantry and Cavalry units. He holds a PhD in Napoleonic History from Florida State University and currently serves as Chief of the Division of Military History at the U.S. Military Academy at West Point. He has appeared frequently on the History Channel.

Why should middle and high school students read about and study America wars? Does doing so promote militarism or instill misguided patriotism? The United States of America was born at war, and the nation has spent the majority of its existence at war. Our wars have demonstrated both the best and worst of who we are. They have freed millions from oppression and slavery, but they have also been a vehicle for fear, racism, and imperialism. Warfare has shaped the geography of our nation, informed our laws, and it even inspired our national anthem. It has united us and it has divided us.

Valley Forge, the USS *Constitution*, Gettysburg, Wounded Knee, Belleau Wood, Normandy, Midway, Inchon, the A Shau Valley, and Fallujah are all a part of who we are as a nation. Therefore, the study of America at war does not necessarily make students or educators militaristic; rather, it makes them thorough and responsible. To ignore warfare, which has been such a significant part of our history, would not only leave our education incomplete, it would also be negligent.

For those who wish to avoid warfare, or to at least limit its horrors, understanding conflict is a worthwhile, and even necessary, pursuit. The American author John Steinbeck once said, "all war is a symptom of man's failure as a thinking animal." If Steinbeck is right, then we must think. And we must think about war. We must study war with all its attendant horrors and miseries. We must study the heroes and the villains. We must study the root causes of our wars, how we chose to fight them, and what has been achieved or lost through them. The study of America at war is an essential component of being an educated American.

Still, there is something compelling in our military history that makes the study not only necessary, but enjoyable, as well. The desperation that drove Washington's soldiers across the Delaware River at the end of 1776 intensifies an exciting story of American success against all odds. The sailors and Marines who planted the American flag on the rocky peak of Mount Suribachi on Iwo Jima still speak to us of courage and sacrifice. The commitment that led American airmen to the relief of West Berlin in the Cold War inspires us to the service of others. The stories of these men and women are exciting, and they matter. We should study them. Moreover, for all the suffering it brings, war has at times served noble purposes for the United States. Americans can find common pride in the chronicle of the Continental Army's few victories and many defeats in the struggle for independence. We can accept that despite inflicting deep national wounds and lingering division, our Civil War yielded admirable results in the abolition of slavery and eventual national unity. We can celebrate American resolve and character as the nation rallied behind a common cause to free the world from tyranny in World War II. We can do all that without necessarily promoting war.

In this series of books, Mason Crest Publishers offers students a foundation for the study of American wars. Building on the expertise of a team of accomplished authors, the series explores the causes, conduct, and consequences of America's wars. It also presents educators with the means to take their students to a deeper understanding of the material through additional research and project ideas. I commend it to all students and to those who educate them to become responsible, informed Americans.

Chapter 1

The Causes of Wars on the Frontier

Throughout the 19th century, people of European descent held varied views of the indigenous peoples of North America. From early times, these Native Americans, sometimes referred to as Indians, were misunderstood or considered wild savages. As the United States grew and expanded westward, Americans would often clash with the Native Americans they encountered. This was especially true during the decades between 1860 and 1890, when a series of wars between Native American tribes and the U.S. military were fought to determine control of the American West.

Native Americans on the Great Plains depended on the bison, or American buffalo, for many everyday necessities. No part of the slaughtered animal was wasted; the Indians ate the meat, used the bones to make tools and weapons, and used the hides to make clothing and shelter. Recognizing this, some white men started killing the animals as a strategy to weaken

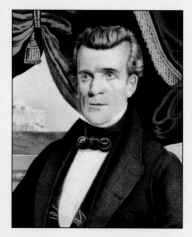

James K. Polk wanted to expand the United States across the North American continent.

An 1800 census showed the U.S. population to be 5.3 million people. The census of 1850 recorded 23.2 million people, a substantial surge in population. These people needed places to live, and because many Americans made their living as farmers during the nineteenth century, they needed large areas of land where they could tend crops and livestock. Such land was not available in the eastern states, which had been settled during the seventeenth and eighteenth centuries. But in the West, there were large tracts of land that were only inhabited by a few people—the Native Americans.

During the first half of the nineteenth century, the United States acquired territory from foreign powers. The 1803 Louisiana Purchase added 530 million acres (210 million ha) to the United States. The U.S. acquired the right to Florida and the Gulf coast from Spain in 1819. The independent country of Texas was annexed by the United States in 1845. After the Mexican War in 1846–1848, the United States secured additional territory in the southwest, including all or part of the present-day states of Arizona, California, Colorado, Kansas, Nevada, New Mexico, Oklahoma, Utah, and Wyoming.

President James K. Polk, who waged the Mexican War, believed in the idea of "manifest destiny," which was shared by many Americans at the time. This was a belief that Americans were destined to control all the

 WORDS TO UNDERSTAND IN THIS CHAPTER

homestead—a place where someone lives. In the West, a white settler who claimed an area of land, built a home, and farmed it for five years was given the land at no charge by the federal government.

ratify—to give formal consent to a treaty or agreement.

treaty—an agreement between two or more parties.

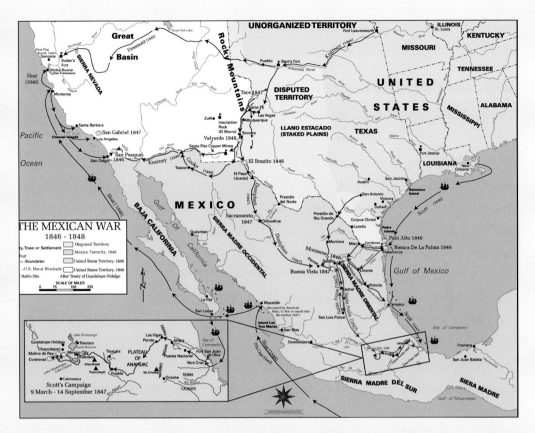

A map showing the American conquest of territory during the Mexican War in 1846-1848. The area of the map labeled Unorganized Territory was designated for Native American tribes that had been pushed from their homes east of the Mississippi River.

continental lands west to the Pacific, south to the Rio Grande, and north to Canada.

A number of other factors contributed to America's pursuit of westward expansion in the latter part of the 19th century. These included the forced relocation of Native American tribes to reservations; gold rushes in Colorado, California, and the Black Hills of South Dakota; and the building of the Transcontinental Railroad. American merchants and farmers saw tremendous opportunities in the westward expansion.

Native Americans did not see the same benefits. However, most Natives disagreed about the proper way to react to the arrival of European Americans. Some thought they should adopt the ways of the white men and live alongside them peacefully. Others were willing to move west, in order to get away from settlers and practice their traditional ways of life in peace. And still others believed the tribe should stay on its traditional lands, and fight to defend its territory.

U.S. Government Policies

The U.S. government recognized the opportunities for settlers expanding into western territories. In fact, one of the reasons that Americans had fought the Revolution was because King George III of Great Britain had prohibited the thirteen British colonies from expanding westward. To maintain peace as white settlers moved west, the government made many promises to the Native American tribes. Unfortunately, many of these promises were eventually broken.

For example, a law called the Northwest Ordinance of 1787 said that the U.S. government would never allow settlement in the tribal lands to the south of the Great Lakes (present-day Illinois, Indiana, Michigan, and Ohio), without the consent of the tribes. However, settlers ignored the restrictions and encroached on Indian land. Soon there was fighting, with the U.S. military sent to protect the settlers. An alliance of Shawnee, Potawatomi, Ottawa, Ojibway, Delaware, and other Great Lakes tribes, led by a chief of the Miami tribe named Little Turtle, won some early victories. Soon, however, the chiefs realized they could not win. There were simply too many soldiers, and they were too well armed.

So Little Turtle and other chiefs took money from the U.S. government in exchange for land. In the Treaty of Greenville, in 1795, the Native

 NATIVE AMERICANS AND LAND OWNERSHIP

Native Americans and white settlers had vastly different perspectives on land ownership. Land ownership was not important to Native Americans. They believed that the lands where they lived were the property of all members of the tribe, and could not be owned by any one person. American settlers, on the other hand, believed in private land ownership. These disparate views prompted the Native American frontier wars, which are often referred to as the longest wars in U.S. history.

Americans agreed to give up their claim to most of Ohio and Indiana.

In 1813–1814, a civil war occurred among the Creek tribe, which lived in western Georgia and Alabama. One faction wanted to live in peace with the Americans. The other, known as the Red Sticks, wanted to fight for their land. In March 1814, General Andrew Jackson led a U.S. army that won a decisive victory over the Red Stick Creeks at Horseshoe Bend in Alabama. Jackson forced the Creeks to sign a peace treaty that gave the United States 23 million acres of land in Alabama and Georgia. Even the Creeks who had remained friendly to the United States were forced to leave their lands under this treaty.

Jackson would eventually become the president of the United States, and on May 28, 1830, he signed into law a bill for the complete removal of Native Americans east of the Mississippi River. The Cherokees and

President Andrew Jackson signed the Indian Removal Act in 1830, which called for eastern tribes to be moved west of the Mississippi River to "Indian Territory" in Oklahoma. No tribes were spared. Even the Cherokee, Chickasaw, Choctaw, Creek, and Seminole nations—often called the "Five Civilized Tribes" by whites—were forced to go.

other tribes that had remained in Georgia were stunned. They had tried to adopt the ways of the Europeans. They had even adopted a constitution modeled on the U.S. Constitution. Had they not been good neighbors?

However, the Americans had another reason for wanting the Cherokee lands in Georgia. Gold had been discovered there. The state of Georgia passed laws making it a crime to discourage Cherokees from leaving the state. When missionaries took the side of the Native Americans, they, too, were thrown in jail. The Cherokees would have to leave. The governor of Georgia divided up their territories and distributed it in a lottery to white Georgians.

Not all white Americans favored the removal of Native Americans. The Indians had some famous defenders in Congress, including Senator Daniel Webster and Senator Henry Clay. In addition, Reverend Samuel

This painting of the Trail of Tears depicts the grueling journey of the Cherokee through five states in 1838–39. At least one-third of the Indians forced to march to Indian Territory did not survive the journey.

Worcester, who was a missionary to the Cherokees in Georgia, went to court over Georgia's attempt to take Indian lands.

When Chief Justice John Marshall ruled that the Cherokees were a sovereign nation in the case *Worcester v. Georgia* (1832), the Cherokees thought they had won, and that their previous treaty would be upheld. However, Georgia state officials ignored the Supreme Court's ruling, and so did President Andrew Jackson. The U.S. government soon began forcibly removing Native Americans. A few hundred Cherokees out of 17,000 signed the Treaty of New Echota in 1835. Even though almost all of the other Cherokees opposed the treaty, the U.S. government used these signatures to justify forced removal of the tribe.

About 3,000 Cherokees were sent on boats to Indian Territory in the West. During the winter of 1838–39, another 14,000 Native Americans were forced to march through Tennessee, Kentucky, Illinois, Missouri, and Arkansas. This event is known as the "Trail of Tears," because thousands of Native Americans died from hunger and illness.

Altogether, about 60,000 Indians were removed from the southeast United States. These included Cherokee, Choctaw, Creek, Chicksaw, and Seminole Indians. Since white Americans continued to move west as well, and Missouri had already become a state by 1821, Indian Territory needed to be moved even further west—Oklahoma.

The Native Americans who remained in the East were pressured to leave. Merchants sued them over phony debts and took their lands. The Native Americans couldn't defend themselves in court because laws had been passed prohibiting them from being legal witnesses. Even Native Americans who had been good neighbors and adopted the ways of the white man were driven west. This was a violation of the Indian Removal Act, which said that Indians could remain if they adopted white man ways. The white Americans simply wanted their lands, so their Native American neighbors were pushed to the west.

Differing Cultures

In most cases, Native American tribes were not set up like governments with a single leader or assembly of leaders. Tribes often had multiple chiefs, so the ones who signed a treaty with the United States might not represent all members of the tribe. Young warriors could be belligerent: they were intent on keeping their culture and saw threats to that culture wherever they turned. Older chiefs often could not control the younger warriors and prevent them from attacking settlers or soldiers that they saw as enemies.

 **INDIAN TERRITORY**

As Native American tribes moved west, the U.S. government assigned a place for them to go. The land to the west that was not already organized as U.S. states or territories was known as Indian Territory. Over time, however, the Indian Territory grew smaller as new U.S. territories and states were formed from those lands. By 1854, the Indian Territory had been reduced to about the size of the present-day state of Oklahoma.

The discovery of gold and other valuable resources in the western territories drew many people into the Native American lands.

Among other factors that compounded the tensions within the Native American tribes at this time were that they were being forced to relocate to unfamiliar lands where other Native Americans tribes had historically lived. The sudden change from hunting to farming imposed on them by the federal government was also a hardship. Buffalo hunting, which had been a mainstay of Native American life on the Great Plains, was virtually eradicated by whites that hunted the buffalo nearly to extinction. Railroad companies hired professional hunters to kill large numbers of buffalo to provide meat for work crews, and sometimes railroad passengers shot the animals simply for sport. The Native American chiefs who signed those treaties during the so-called "frontier wars" era often did not fully understand all the treaty terms.

Native Americans also were unaware that it took a long time for the U.S. government to *ratify* a treaty. They thought that promised payments and supplies under a treaty were being delayed on purpose.

Settlers and those who traveled through the Native American territories in the West often did not know or care much about federal policies toward Native Americans. They did not believe the Native Americans had rights to the land.

Difficulties with Treaties

During the 1830s and 1840s, American settlers traveled west through the Great Plains and other Indian territories on the Oregon Trail and other routes. Journalists sometimes reported about cruel native tribes massacring white people, and Native Americans did indeed kill some settlers. But Native Americans also helped settlers cross the Great Plains. They sold the white people food, and acted as messengers between wagon trains.

Things began to change with the discovery of gold at Sutter's Mill in California in 1848. The California gold rush drew tens of thousands of people to the west, looking to exploit the mineral wealth of this region. Soon, settlers moved into Native American hunting grounds. Since the Native Americans had lived and hunted on these lands for centuries, they resented being pushed away. Violence soon erupted.

In 1851, the U.S. government met with the leaders of several Native American tribes on the Great Plains. They agreed to the Treaty of Fort Laramie, in which each Native American tribe agreed to live within a bounded territory, allowed the U.S. government to construct roads through and forts in that territory, and agreed not to attack settlers passing through their lands. The Native American lands became known as reservations, because they were supposed to be "reserved" for the tribes.

Fort Laramie was an important trading post in Wyoming, where the Laramie River and the North Platte River meet. American leaders on the frontier signed several treaties with Great Plains tribes at the fort.

In return, the United States agreed to honor the boundaries of each tribe's territory and pay the Native American tribes an annual fee of $50,000, a significant amount at that time. The Cheyenne, Sioux, Arapaho, Assiniboine, Mandan, Gros Ventre, and Arihara tribes who signed the treaty also agreed to end hostilities among their tribes.

However, the peace did not last. The United States failed to control the number of settlers who flooded into the Native Americans' territory. They also did not always make the payments or live up to other promises made in the Treaty of Fort Laramie. Dishonest agents from the Bureau of Indian Affairs sometimes stole supplies that were supposed to go to the tribes. Native Americans grew angry at the federal government's constant demand for more of their land.

During the 1860s, further aspects of life changed for Native American tribes. For instance, the U.S. government wanted the tribes of the Great Plains to give up their traditional nomadic ways, including buffalo hunting, and settle down as farmers in the same way that white settlers did.

Under restrictions imposed by the Indian Peace Commission, each tribe was required to settle on a government-controlled reservation, which was to have a limited and defined boundary. It was usually the land where the tribe already hunted and had settled, but not always. Sometimes a tribe had to move to another reservation. Government officials promised that they would give the Native Americans whatever food they could not grow or produce for themselves. Separate treaties were negotiated with each tribe.

Settlers with a covered wagon pause for a photo on the Great Plains in Nebraska's Loup Valley.

Troubles Begin

During the 1860s and 1870s, problems emerged when the settlers started moving into the Native Americans' territories. Settlers began to take over land in the Great Plains, particularly in what is now Texas, New Mexico, Colorado, Wyoming, and Montana. They built homes and farms in Oklahoma, Kansas, Nebraska, and North and South Dakota. The Sioux and other tribes, including the Crow, Pawnee, and Arapaho, were pushed back so that **homesteaders** could put down roots.

A trail of dead bison in the snow, circa 1872. Hunters would kill the animals and take only the hide, which was used to make warm robes. They often left the meat to rot—an act that shocked Native Americans who relied on the animals for food.

What started as disgruntlement on both sides soon turned into conflicts and then outright battles. The Native Americans refused to let themselves be conquered. Conflicts, skirmishes, and battles continued for years between the United States and all the native tribes, as they fought back against those who were pushing them off their land and threatening their cultural identity. Treaties were regularly forged, put in place, but then disregarded by the U.S. government.

The Settlers' Plans

The land on which the Native Americans had relied became land that the settlers farmed. They grew their own crops. Buffalo, which were a mainstay of Native American hunting, were killed by the settlers nearly to extinction. The Native Americans depended on the animals they hunted so that they could turn them into food, fashion their clothing and tools, and build shelters for themselves and their families. The tepees they lived in were made from buffalo skins. Native Americans used other parts of the buffalo to make cooking containers and tools.

Soon, the new homesteaders discovered another way to use the animal products. Buffalo robes became quite fashionable. Lined and unlined robes and coats were widely advertised, even in the East. At a Boston store, buffalo robes were sold for as little as $9.

On average, a white commercial hunter could kill 100 animals a day. Buffalo hunting not only provided food and clothing for the new settlers. Hides and bones from the buffalo were ground into fertilizer, which was another reason the settlers slaughtered the animals.

The buffalo were getting fewer in number. Hunting was not the only cause of the buffalo's decline. Climate change and drought on the Great Plains also figured in what was to become the demise of the buffalo.

What the Native Americans had enjoyed for so long—the buffalo hunt—was becoming just a distant memory. On a typical Native American buffalo hunt, a mass of hunters on horseback charged into a buffalo herd. Yells of the Native Americans would fill the air, as swirling clouds of dust covered the Plains. With arrows bringing the buffalo down, the Native Americans captured their game. But with the decline of the buffalo population, this key element of Native American culture was no longer available.

 ## TEXT-DEPENDENT QUESTIONS

1. Why did U.S. settlers want to seize the land that belonged to the Native Americans?
2. What was one species of animal both the settlers and Native Americans felt it was very important for them to hunt?

 ## RESEARCH PROJECT

Pick a tool or weapon used by the Native Americans that people would have little use for today, and explain why this is so.

Chapter 2

Reservation Life

Beginning in the first half of the 19th century, federal policy stated that certain tribes had to be confined to a particular area of land, known as a reservation, where they could maintain their traditional ways of life. How did the Native Americans feel about this? They resented being forcibly relocated and deprived of life on their historic lands. Tribes of Native Americans were nomadic; this was the basis of their economic life. But now they were restricted to a particular area, not of their own choosing. In addition, tribes hostile to each other were now forced to live in close proximity.

A crowd of Native Americans watch as a steer is slaughtered and butchered to provide part of the reservation's monthly ration of beef.

In practice, treaties rarely benefitted Native Americans. Their provisions were confusing. The lives of Native Americans on the reservations were far worse than how they had lived before the settlers arrived. Although they no longer needed to provide for their own food, clothing, or shelter, taking these responsibilities away from the Native Americans undermined the way of life these people had always known.

Initially, setting up reservations was viewed as a positive strategy and a positive change in how the federal government viewed the Native Americans. Rather than ignoring the Native Americans, the U.S. government believed it was now taking an active role in ensuring their welfare. However, from the Native Americans' perspective the government did not have the Indians' best interests at heart. It seemed instead that they wanted to confine the Native Americans so that they would not be able to launch raids on white settlers.

Although the causes of the frontier wars are complex, one of the major reasons these conflicts erupted was that the Native Americans were forced to accept something they did not want—reservations—and they rebelled.

Native Americans received food *rations* through tickets. If a family didn't have tickets, they did not get food. Clothing was not plentiful, and they did not like the clothing they received from the federal government. Farmers, teachers, and missionaries tried to get the Native Americans to accept their ways of life, but those ways of life held no appeal, and these approaches failed.

Battle of Punished Woman Fork

One clash broke out in 1878 partly as a result of a lack of rations, and disease brought on by starvation. The Battle of Punished Woman Fork

WORDS TO UNDERSTAND IN THIS CHAPTER

parley—a conference or discussion between enemies.
rations—a regular allowance of food.

A Native American family poses in western clothes outside of an adobe home on their California reservation. The U.S. government encouraged Native Americans to give up their culture and adopt the same way of life as the white settlers who moved into their lands.

involved the Northern Cheyenne, who had been living on the Cheyenne-Arapaho reservation in Oklahoma. Angered over how little food they received, the tribe fled from the reservation, determined to return to their home territory. As they made their way 1,500 miles (2,415 km) north to the Kansas Territory, fleeing from pursuing soldiers, the Native Americans traveled through dangerous canyons, including one called Punished Woman Fork. Their plan was to hide during daytime and continue their escape at nighttime, under the leadership of Chiefs Dull Knife and Little Wolf. A total of 92 warriors, 120 women, and 141 children were in the group.

Lieutenant Colonel William H. Lewis, along with a militia of 238 soldiers, was dispatched to capture and return the Cheyenne to the reservation. Lewis and his soldiers caught up to the Native Americans. While the women, children, and the elderly hid, the warriors fought, wounding Lewis, who eventually died from his wounds. The Cheyenne then escaped. Several other soldiers were wounded. The Cheyenne lost 60 horses, many of their possessions, and much of their food. Reliable casualty statistics for both sides are unknown. The remaining soldiers rounded up the Cheyenne and returned them to the reservation.

Native Americans' Complaints

A major complaint on the reservations was that the settlers had ruined the old ways of the Native Americans once they began hunting and slaughtering buffalo. As noted previously, much of the Native Americans' livelihood depended on buffalo. The Native Americans were furious that the white men were hunting buffalo for sport, and their answer at first was to conduct raids on white settlements.

The Native Americans found that land on the reservations was often unsuitable for farming. Also, the Native Americans were not knowledgeable about irrigation and most of their attempts at farming failed.

Not all Native American groups accepted the U.S. reservations decrees. The Modoc was a small tribe that lived in what today is southern Oregon and northern California. They resisted when the U.S. government tried to force them to share a reservation with their longtime enemies, the Klamath tribe. Led by a chief named Kintpuash, or "Captain Jack," the Modocs fought against the U.S. government during the 1870s. The small band of about 150 Modoc hid in caves and on rocky plateaus. Eventually, Captain Jack and some of his warriors were captured, and the rest surren-

A Teton Sioux family stands outside their tepee on a reservation in the Great Plains.

THE MODOC WAR, 187 -1873

The Modoc tribe was located on the West Coast, at the border of California and Oregon. They had signed a treaty with American authorities in 1864, which ceded their lands and settled them on a reservation with Klamaths in Oregon. The two tribes did not get along, and the Modocs went back to where they had once lived. However, white settlers had moved into this region by this time, and they wanted the Modocs to go back to the reservation. This was the only major Native American war fought in California, and the only one in which a general of the regular army was killed.

Under orders of the Bureau of Indian Affairs, troops were sent from Fort Klamath to move the Modocs, by force if necessary. As troops burned their villages, the Modocs fled.

There were 60 Modoc fighters and approximately 600 U.S. troops. The battles occurred in a countryside covered by sagebrush, with lava plateaus and wooded mountains. The Modocs had settled along the shores of Tule Lake and Lost River. The terrain was rugged and uneven, with caves accessible for hiding.

A trail through the rocky area known as Captain Jack's Stronghold, where the Modoc hid from the U.S. Army.

The U.S. Army increased their pressure tactics against the Modoc tribe, and insisted on their full surrender. The Army also wanted to declare them prisoners of war. The Modocs demanded their own reservation on Lost River, as well as amnesty.

A U.S. Army general, Edward Canby, visited the Modoc leaders in April 1873 hoping to arrange a peace treaty. Instead, Canby was murdered by the Modoc leader Captain Jack. The Modoc tribe had resolved to fight to the death to defend their land from Captain Jack's stronghold near Tule Lake. The fighting continued until May 10, when the Modoc were defeated. The last of the band surrendered in June 1873. Captain Jack and others were tried and executed for their role in Canby's murder. Other Modocs received amnesty but sent to new lands in Oklahoma.

dered. Captain Jack was executed by the government for murdering two Americans during a *parley*; the rest of his band was sent to the Indian Territory, where they were kept as prisoners of war until 1909. Today, the Modoc have a small territory in Oklahoma.

Life on the Reservation

As some buffalo-skin tepees wore out, Native Americans had to move to log cabins. In the 1880s, permanent houses like log cabins mostly replaced tepees on the reservations.

While Native Americans plied trades such as basketry, fishing for salmon canneries, and selling medicinal cascara bark, the U.S. government wanted them to learn skills and attitudes that the government felt were necessary for success as American citizens. To acquire these skills and attitudes, many Native American children were forcibly sent away from their homes to boarding schools, located hundreds of miles away from their families and friends. Here they studied, as U.S. children did, reading, writing, and arithmetic. The result? Relationships between Native American children and their parents suffered, leading to family breakdown.

A Native American farmer plows his land on a reservation in Arizona.

View of a U.S. school for Native American children on the Pine Ridge Reservation in South Dakota, 1891.

Cows, horses, and chickens had been promised to Native Americans when they were moved to reservations. In reality, they did not get all that had been promised.

The United States sent farming instructors to the reservations. While this was presented a positive, vital learning experience for the Native Americans, it turned out that this was just another way that their culture was becoming diminished.

Instruction Controversy

Conservative, traditional Native Americans, for example those from the Teton Sioux tribe, also known as the Lakota, did not want instructors around. They threatened the instructors with death.

At first, by way of resistance, conservative chiefs complained to the U.S. government. To keep peace and placate the Native Americans, agents from the Bureau of Indian Affairs let Native American leaders, rather than the agents themselves, distribute food to their own people. The Lakota people accepted this, seeing it as an example of generosity and gift giving.

It was the duty of the head of the family to personally pick up his family's rations. Although this could be seen as an honor for him, it usually was a hardship, as the rations were dropped off far from his home. Because the head of the family was not always at home, farming tended to fall by the wayside. Repairs had to be made to tools and equipment. This often did not happen.

Benefits for Native Americans

While the arrival of U.S. settlers had disrupted the way of life of the Native Americans, Americans leaders of the nineteenth century believed that their presence also benefited the Native Americans in certain ways. For example, metal tools and weapons like firearms made it easier for the Native Americans to support themselves. Supposedly, they were then able to spend more time on food gathering, religious observance, and recreation. It did not always work out that way, though.

The possibility of an easier life did not make up for everything the Native Americans had lost in the westward expansion. The disruptions of their way of life and the threat to their very existence led to a series of conflicts and battles with the U.S. Army, beginning in the 1860s and lasting through 1890.

 TEXT-DEPENDENT QUESTIONS

1. Why did the Northern Cheyenne leave their reservation in 1878?
2. Why did many Native American attempts to establish farms on their reservations fail?
3. What were three of the supposed benefits of reservation life?

 **RESEARCH PROJECT**

The Modocs went into hiding because they were not willing to put up with suffering on reservations. Write a short essay about what their lives were like when they hid out in caves.

Chapter 3

Warfare in the Southwest

In the American Southwest, Native Americans often fought against Mexican authorities. Once control over the territory passed to the United States after the Mexican War, U.S. troops were responsible for preventing hostile warriors from crossing the border to attack American settlers in the region.

The Apache were one of the most powerful tribes in this region along the U.S.-Mexico border. When the war with Mexico began in 1846, Apache chief Mangas Coloradas agreed to let U.S. troops pass safely through Apache lands. When the war ended Mangas Coloradas signed a peace treaty with U.S. authori-

African-American cavalry troopers known as "Buffalo Soldiers" played a crucial role in the long and difficult search for the Apache chief Victorio and his followers. They trailed the Apache band deep into unfamiliar territory in 1879 and 1880.

ties. The Mexicans had often fought the Apaches, so they were happy to be rid of them. The peace lasted until the late 1850s, when gold miners began to arrive in the Pinos Altos mountains of New Mexico. In 1860, after a group of miners attacked an Apache settlement, Mangas Coloradas began to launch raids against American settlements in Texas.

Mangas Coloradas was captured and killed by American forces in 1863, but other Apaches continued the fight. One was his son-in-law Cochise, who was chief of another Apache tribe, the Chokonen Apache.

The Navajo War of the 1860s

The Apache were not the only tribe along the border to fight with the Americans. In what today is New Mexico, the Navaho chief Manuelito had made treaties with the whites. However, when the army killed Navaho livestock because the animals came on pastures that the soldiers said belonged to them, the Navaho began to raid the Army's livestock and supply trains. Fighting grew worse, and after a Navaho attack on Fort Defiance on April 30, 1860, more soldiers were sent to the area to hunt down the Navaho warriors, as well as the Apache. The soldiers were unable to catch them, and both sides soon became weary of fighting. A peace treaty was signed in February of 1861.

General James Carleton arrived in New Mexico with his troops in the spring of 1862. Carleton had come to fight Confederate soldiers, but the Confederates had left the area. Carleton decided he would fight the Apaches and Navaho instead. He ordered that no talks were to take place with the Native Americans and that all Native American men were to be killed. Any survivors were to be sent to a reservation at Bosque Redondo.

First Carleton concentrated on the Mescelero Apaches. By spring of

WORDS TO UNDERSTAND IN THIS CHAPTER

neutralize—to render something ineffective or harmless.
superintendent—a person who oversees or is in charge.

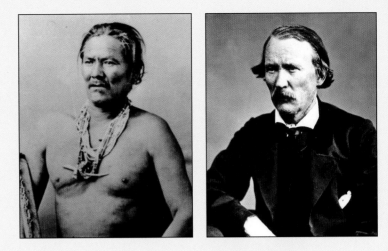

Kit Carson (right) was a reluctant, though highly effective, Indian fighter. He used merciless tactics to force the Navaho led by Manuelito (left) to settle on a reservation at Bosque Redondo.

1863, most of them had been killed, fled the country, or had been relocated on the reservation. Cochise managed to avoid capture with a small band of warriors, and he would continue his raids for the next decade. However, with the Apache threat **neutralized** Carleton turned his attention to the Navaho. He gave them until July 20 to give themselves up but none did.

Carleton then ordered Kit Carson and soldiers under his command to destroy all of the crops and livestock of the Navaho. In October, some of the Navaho surrendered and were sent to Bosque Redondo. During the early months of 1864, Kit Carson and his men pursued the Navaho in their mountain hideouts. The Navaho were starving, and within a few months, many more had surrendered. They were marched to Bosque Redondo in freezing weather and snowstorms. Hundreds died along the way. By the spring of 1864, around 8,500 Apaches and Navaho had been sent to the reservation.

Those who made it to Bosque Redondo may have wished they hadn't. They did not have enough clothing, food, blankets, or firewood. The 1864 crop at Bosque failed, and starvation and disease killed many of the Navahos. Those who could escaped. So many were fleeing the reservation that by the fall of 1865, Carleton ordered that every Navaho found off the reservation should be killed. The crops at Bosque failed again in 1865, and the Indians were given food that had been found unfit for soldiers to eat. More Indians died.

The Comanche warrior Quanah Parker formed an alliance with the Kiowa and Cheyenne to attack settlers in Texas. The Comanche were the last tribe native to the region known as Llano Estacado ("Staked Plains") to accept reservation life.

Manuelito finally surrendered in the fall of 1866. Soon after that, a new **superintendent** was appointed for the reservation and declared it unfit for living. New reservation lands were given to the Indians closer to their old homes.

Red River War, 1874–1875

One treaty that the U.S. government went back on sparked a war in 1874–1875. Called the Red River War, this armed conflict broke out in northern Texas against Arapaho, Comanche, Cheyenne, and Kiowa tribes. In the Treaty of Medicine Lodge of 1867, the government had promised to issue rations to those tribes and to protect them from aggressive actions by settlers. Instead, rations came slowly, or not at all. White outlaws entered the Native Americans' territory, stole their goods, and went unpunished. To avenge themselves for the loss of rations and the injustices perpetrated by the outlaws, the Native Americans launched raids against the settlers. After a number of bloody incidents in Texas, Kansas, and the Indian Territory (which covered much of the present-day state of Oklahoma), the federal government organized counterattacks. These attacks defeated the Kiowa, Comanche, and Cheyenne tribes, and they drifted back to their reservations.

The largest battle of the war came in September 1874 at Palo Duro Canyon. U.S. troops surprised a large village. Although few warriors were killed, the Americans captured most of their food and horses. This was true of many other battles, leaving the Native Americans starving due to lack of resources.

The Red River War ended in June 1875 when Quanah Parker surrendered his Comanche warriors at Fort Sill, Oklahoma. and surrendered; they were the last large roaming band of southwestern Indians.

Approximately 72 captured Comanche chiefs were kept as prisoners of war in Florida until 1878. The southern buffalo herd become extinct, and northern Texas was opened up to settlement by pioneers even

The Native Americans objected to being forced to relinquish land that had been theirs for generations. A major cause of their anger was that the new settlers, in taking over their territories, destroyed their way of life and undermined their culture.

The settlers seized the Native American peoples' land and killed the animals they found on that land. The animals had been key sources of food and clothing for the Native Americans. But the Native Americans refused to give up what they needed for their survival without a fight.

Victorio's War

When the U.S. government tried to force the Warm Spring Apache tribe onto a reservation in August 1879, their leader, Chief Victorio, fled with an estimated 300 Apaches, including women, children, and old people. They quickly disappeared into the rocky, dangerous Black Range of southern New Mexico.

In order to feed his people, Victorio raided farms throughout the region, sometimes killing people. The newspapers published sensational reports of the murders. The U.S. cavalry was assigned to track Victorio down. They tracked the Apache band through the Arizona and New Mexico countryside. The terrain was brutally difficult to travel—blistering desert sun and no water for miles on end; rocky canyons and cold, windy mountaintops; and a border with Mexico that Victorio would slip across just as the American troops seemed on the verge of capturing him. Mexican authorities refused to allow American troops to cross the border and fight on their territory. However, the Mexicans were hunting the Apaches as well.

The Apache chief Victorio was a great guerrilla fighter who waged war in the blazing deserts and rugged mountains of New Mexico, Arizona, and Texas. U.S. Army officers respected him so much they studied his tactics.

Geronimo (mounted, left) and the Apache chief Naiche (mounted, right) the son of Cochise, fought together in 1886 before being forced to surrender to the U.S. Army. Geronimo's son Perico is standing on the left, holding the famous warrior's grandson.

African-American troops of the Ninth and Tenth Cavalries played a critical role in chasing Victorio. When they heard that the Apaches had crossed the border into Texas again, they stationed guards at all the water holes and mountain passes. They skirmished with the Apaches at Rattlesnake Canyon and other places.

On October 18, 1880, Victorio was killed by Mexican soldiers. His death brought peace along the border. There were still a few small bands of bitterly determined Apache warriors, but they were soon killed or captured.

Conflict with Geronimo

Geronimo, whose Native American name was Goyathlay, was a member of the Chiricahua Apache tribe. He was the last of the great Apache war leaders, though he was technically not a chief of his tribe.

Geronimo was feared by both Americans and Mexicans. In 1858, Mexican soldiers had killed his mother, his wife, and his children. For the rest of his life, Geronimo sought revenge for these deaths against Mexicans.

GENERAL NELSON MILES

When the American Civil War began, Nelson Miles was a storekeeper. He volunteered for military duty, and soon proved to be a capable leader. By the end of the war, Miles had been promoted to the rank of general. After the war ended, he stayed in the U.S. Army, where he participated in many major conflicts of the frontier wars.

In 1874, Miles led an expedition against the Native Americans of the Texas Panhandle. With one battalion and four companies of the Fifth Infantry, two battalions of the Sixth Cavalry, a detachment of artillery, and a company of Delaware Indians, he marched into Camp Supply in Indian Territory and set up operations for his Panhandle campaign.

During the 1874–1875 Red River War, Miles led a column against the Native Americans of the Southern Plains. He then successfully defeated Crazy Horse and his Sioux followers in an 1877 campaign. His troops were also successful that year in battles against Chief Joseph's Nez Perce tribe.

In 1880, Miles was promoted to brigadier general. In 1886, he accepted Geronimo's surrender. In 1890, as major general, he supervised the troops that massacred a small band of Sioux at Wounded Knee. By 1895, Miles had attained the highest military rank—general in chief of the Army.

During 1868, Geronimo battled a rival Apache subgroup, as well as the hated Mexicans. He joined Cochise and other Apaches who resisted white and Hispanic encroachment.

For a while, Geronimo went back and forth on raiding expeditions. During June and July of 1875, he and about 40 followers left the San Carlos Reservation. They killed about 20 settlers in raids, and stole more than 200 head of cattle. Geronimo led another raid into Mexico to steal cattle in May 1883.

When Geronimo left the reservation again in 1885 and headed to Mexico, U.S. forces were sent to capture him. U.S. troops commanded by General George Crook played a game of hide-and-seek along the U.S.-Mexico border. Geronimo surrendered to Crook in 1886, but then fled. A new leader, General Nelson A. Miles, was sent to find the Apache chief. In September 1886, Geronimo surrendered to Miles and was taken to Florida as a prisoner of war for a few years. After being released, Geronimo became a farmer and raised livestock and produce.

The capture of Geronimo marked the end of the 35-year-long Apache Wars. But other conflicts with Native Americans were still being fought on the Great Plains.

 TEXT-DEPENDENT QUESTIONS

1. Why did Mangas Coloradas begin to launch raids against American settlements in Texas?
2. What measures was Kit Carson ordered to take against the Navajo in New Mexico?
3. What 1867 treaty did the U.S. government fail to live up to, sparking the Red River War?

 **RESEARCH PROJECT**

Using the Internet or your school library, learn more about the tribes of the American Southwest, such as the Kiowa, Comanche, Apache, and Navajo. Choose a tribe, and write a two-page report about its history. With what other Native American tribes did it have rivalries or alliances? What are some distinguishing characteristics of the tribe's culture? Share your report with the class.

Chapter 4

Warfare on the Plains during the 1860s

The largest western tribe was the Sioux. The tribe was divided into different groups. The Santee Sioux lived in the woodlands of Minnesota. The Teton Sioux, also known as the Lakota, lived on the Great Plains along with the Cheyennes and other tribes.

The Santee Sioux had been dealing with the white men for some time. Treaties had been signed in which 90 percent of Santee land had been given to the whites. This land, known as the Dakota Territory, included the present-day states of North Dakota, South Dakota, and Minnesota. During the decade before

This oil painting depicts the Sand Creek Massacre, in which Arapaho and Cheyenne Indians were brutally attacked by American soldiers. The battle took place in their camp at Sand Creek in November 1864.

Santee Sioux warriors attack the settlement at New Ulm, Minnesota, in the summer of 1862. The starving Sioux were angry because they had not received rations promised by the U.S. government.

the Civil War more than 150,000 whites had settled in Santee country. The Santees were in debt, their crops had failed, most of the game was gone from the reservation lands, and traders had cheated them.

When a U.S. government payment that was due the Santees didn't arrive in the summer of 1862, the tribe was unable to buy food. Their people were starving. On August 4, 1862, 500 desperate Santees stormed a warehouse in Minnesota. A fight was avoided, however, and the U.S. agent promised Chief Little Crow that food would be released to the Santees from another warehouse 30 miles away.

However, the traders at the other warehouse would not issue food on credit. The Santees were very angry. Then, a few days later, a few hotheaded Santees killed some white settlers. The Santees expected that all the Indians would be punished for this deed and decided to strike first.

 ## WORDS TO UNDERSTAND IN THIS CHAPTER

influx—a coming in, for example, of a group to a community.
massacre—the act of brutally killing helpless or unresisting people.
mutilate—To cut off or permanently destroy; to make imperfect.
stagecoach—a horse-drawn passenger and mail vehicle that ran on a
    regular schedule between established stops.

The Santees, led by Little Crow, killed 20 men and took the food from the storehouse. Then they attacked Fort Ridgely and the town of New Ulm. The Santee braves killed hundreds of settlers along the Minnesota River. They wanted to drive the settlers out of their territory. By this time, Minnesota's Governor Alexander Ramsey had announced to the citizens of Minnesota that "the Sioux Indians must be exterminated or forever driven beyond the borders of this state."

The U.S. Army was engaged in the civil war, but troops commanded by Colonel Henry Sibley were sent to the Dakota Territory. The Santee chiefs decided they were not strong enough to defeat Sibley and his men. Either they would have to surrender, or they would have to leave their territory and live with the Teton Sioux on the Great Plains. Little Crow decided to live with the Plains Indians. He would be killed later when he returned to Minnesota to steal horses.

About 2,000 Santees remained when Sibley marched into their camp and demanded their surrender. The 600 adult males were chained together and put in prison. Then they were sent to court, and 303 were sentenced to death. Before executing them, General John Pope sent the cases to President Abraham Lincoln for his approval. Lincoln had the cases reviewed and found only 39 cases were sufficient to merit execution.

The government took the remaining lands of the Santee Sioux, and the tribe was sent to live at a reservation on Crow Creek in the Dakota

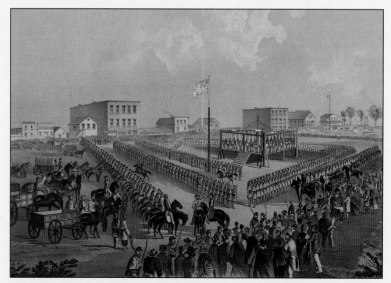

This illustration shows settlers and U.S. soldiers attending the execution of 39 Santee Sioux warriors who had been the ringleaders of the 1862 insurrection in Minnesota. It was the largest mass execution in American history.

Territory. The soil there was poor, there was no game, and the water was bad. About 300 of the 1,300 Santee Sioux sent there in 1863 died during the first winter.

The Sand Creek Massacre

Tensions were also high among the Cheyenne and whites in the Colorado Territory. Gold had been discovered there in 1858, leading to an *influx* of settlers who encroached on Native American hunting grounds. In May 1864, a Cheyenne chief named Lean Bear was killed in an encounter with American soldiers. Fighting broke out, but the leading chief of the Cheyenne, Black Kettle, persuaded his people to stop fighting. Black Kettle sent a message to the authorities in Denver that the Cheyenne did not want a war. However, the governor of the Colorado Territory had already decided that peace was not an option.

Black Kettle and other chiefs met with U.S. Army officers. They were told they had to surrender. Soon after that Black Kettle and his followers made their way toward the U.S. outpost at Fort Lyon. Members of the Arapaho tribe who had ridden with Black Kettle set up a camp near the fort and began receiving rations from the army. Black Kettle's Cheyennes set up camp at Sand Creek, 40 miles (64 km) from Fort Lyon.

The commander at Fort Lyon, Major Scott J. Anthony, insisted that the Arapaho surrender their weapons. He told Black Kettle that as long as the Cheyenne stayed at Sand Creek, they would be safe. He even gave the chief an American flag to fly over his lodge, to show that the Cheyenne were peaceful and should not be attacked.

On the morning of November 29, 1864, there were about 800 Indians camped with Black Kettle at Sand Creek. Two-thirds of them were women and children, because most of the male warriors were away from the camp hunting for food. About 700 members of the First Colorado Volunteer Regiment, led by Colonel John M. Chivington, attacked the camp by surprise. Women and children were slaughtered, and their bodies were *mutilated*. Many of the

John Chivington was condemned for ordering his troops to massacre peaceful Cheyenne at Sand Creek.

Native Americans, including Black Kettle, were able to escape, but the soldiers killed 133 Indians, more than 100 of them women and children.

In his report of the battle, Chivington claimed that he had attacked a large, well-armed band of Native Americans and won a decisive victory. At first Chivington and his men were praised as heroes. But soon the authorities learned more details about what actually happened at Sand Creek. The federal government launched an investigation into the *massacre*,

CHEYENNE PEACEMAKER BLACK KETTLE

Black Kettle was a chief of the Cheyenne. He is believed to have been born sometime between 1807 and 1812. Many accounts of his life refer to Black Kettle as a peace-loving leader. In his dealings with the United States, he struggled with decisions that would keep his people from resisting and sought peaceful solutions through diplomacy with the United States.

Black Kettle was married four times, and fathered at least 17 children.

He was camped with a small band of followers at Sand Creek, where he was attacked in 1864. Black Kettle and his people had moved to the area under the Fort Wise Treaty, anticipating that they would be protected by the U.S. military. Under another treaty, a year later, Black Kettle moved to still another reservation in Kansas.

His main concern was for the well-being of his people and for this reason they moved from reservation to reservation. These decisions have been called foolish, as promises by the U.S. government were broken time and again. For example, food and supplies never arrived at an Oklahoma reservation where Black Kettle and the Cheyenne settled, forcing them to leave and find food to keep from starving.

In 1868, Black Kettle, hoping once more for peace, tried to surrender at Fort Cobb, Oklahoma. Major General William B. Hazen said that Black Kettle was not authorized to make peace. One week after Hazen's talk with Black Kettle, General Custer led the 700-man Seventh Cavalry to the peaceful Cheyenne camp on the Washita River, where they surrounded it. A fight broke out, in which 103 Native Americans, including Black Kettle, and 15 U.S. soldiers were killed.

Black Kettle was buried in an unmarked grave. His bones and jewelry were discovered in 1934.

The Powder River country is an area of the Great Plains located between the Bighorn Mountains of Montana and Wyoming and the Black Hills of South Dakota.

and Chivington was reprimanded for his part in the attack.

The Sand Creek Massacre ruined any chance of peace. Cheyenne, Arapaho, and Sioux warriors began attacking wagon trains and small military posts. They destroyed telegraphs and killed white settlers. However, they knew they would have to leave Colorado. Most of them decided to go north to join the Teton Sioux and the Northern Cheyenne. Black Kettle continued to refuse to fight. He and his followers went to live south of the Arkansas River.

The Powder River Invasion

West of the Black Hills of the Dakotas, in Wyoming and Montana, was Powder River country. This was a stronghold of the Teton Sioux. The Cheyenne, Shoshone, and Arapaho tribes lived in this region, also. The Indians in Powder River country were surprised when U.S. soldiers decided to invade the territory.

In July 1865, General Patrick E. Connor led an invasion of the Powder River country. He divided his force, with one group of his men sent to build Fort Connor. This fort was intended to protect settlers traveling on the Bozeman Trail, a new route to Oregon that passed directly through the Sioux lands in Montana. Then he took part of his troops and surprised a group of Arapaho, destroying their village and capturing one-third of their horses.

The other 2,000 soldiers marched along the Powder River. When they approached a large village, the Sioux, Cheyenne, and Arapaho warriors living there decided to attack before the soldiers could arrive. On September 8, 1865, the warriors charged at the American column. They soldiers were outnumbered American, but they fought bravely.

In one notable incident, a Cheyenne war chief named Roman Nose told his warriors not to charge until he had made the troops empty their guns shooting at him. Then Roman Nose rode his horse directly at the front line of U.S. soldiers. When he was close enough to see their faces, he rode from one end of the line to the other and back again as they fired at him. Roman Nose was not hit, but his horse was killed. At that point, the Native American warriors charged. However, the Americans had two small cannons, which they used to beat back the attack.

The Cheyenne leader Roman Nose defies American soldiers during a battle. Roman Nose was considered one of the greatest of the Cheyenne war chiefs.

General Patrick Connor was a veteran of the Civil War, but his tactics failed to stop Native American attacks on the Bozeman Trail.

All that night and the next day it snowed. The American soldiers were low on food and not healthy. There wasn't enough grass and water for their horses. On September 10, the Americans left their camp and began to retreated out of the Powder River region. The Native Americans came out to watch the soldiers leave. Although there was some skirmishing, the warriors allowed the soldiers to leave without forcing an all-out battle. The soldiers soon rejoined General Connor's force, and left the region for Utah.

The Powder River expedition was a failure, because it did not stop attacks on settlers using the Bozeman Trail. In fact, the attacks became even more intense over the next few years, as Native Americans grew more determined to prevent whites from passing through their lands.

Warfare in Kansas

Roman Nose returned to Kansas in early 1866 to hunt, even though chiefs had given these lands by treaty to the whites. Roman Nose's leadership during the Powder River expedition gave him great prestige among the Cheyenne and Arapaho peoples. When a *stagecoach* line was opened in Kansas that ran straight through the best buffalo ranges, Roman Nose and his warriors told the company they would start raiding if the stagecoaches continued. Then Roman Nose settled into camp to wait for spring.

Soldiers led by General Winfield Scott Hancock were soon headed for Kansas. Hancock demanded that Roman Nose meet with him, but Roman Nose refused. Finally, Hancock marched troops to Roman Nose's camp. Roman Nose sent the women and children away, met with Hancock, and promised to bring his people back to the American camp. However, he and his warriors escaped. Hancock sent troops to Roman Nose's abandoned camp and destroyed everything there.

In revenge, Roman Nose and his warriors began raided stagecoach stations, attacked railroads, and ripped out telegraph lines. More than 75 settlers were killed in attacks on farms and ranches. However, other

At the Battle of Beecher's Island, a war party of 600 Cheyenne, Sioux, and Arapahos attacked a small contingent of American scouts.

Indians submitted to the U.S. Army and were sent to reservations.

In 1868, General Philip Sheridan took command of soldiers in Kansas's forts and tried to hunt down Roman Nose and his band of about 300 warriors. In the fall of 1868, at the battle of Beecher's Island near the Kansas-Colorado border, Roman Nose was killed. His death was a great blow to the Cheyenne's hope of defending their lands.

Sheridan believed a winter campaign would be successful. The Native Americans would be attacked in their permanent winter camps. Since they were all in one place, rather than scattered, Sheridan thought that by destroying their food supplies and shelter, and putting the women and children at the mercy of the Army and the elements, the Native Americans would have no choice but to surrender. For many officers, this strategy raised moral questions, which never were resolved.

Sheridan's attack plan involved three columns of soldiers converging on the Native American winter grounds near the Texas Panhandle: one from Fort Lyon in Colorado, one from Camp Supply in what is now Oklahoma, and one from Fort Bascom in New Mexico. This major campaign was fought by Lieutenant Colonel George Armstrong Custer's

Seventh Cavalry. It was a fierce, miles-long battle, during which Custer, at nighttime withdrew from the field, taking as prisoners 53 women and children. The Seventh Cavalry lost 21 officers and soldiers killed in the Battle of Washita. The estimate of Native American deaths was more than 100 killed, many of them women and children.

Red Cloud's War

During the first part of 1866, the government tried to get the important Sioux warrior chief Red Cloud to sign a treaty at Fort Laramie. For a

Red Cloud (inset) was the leader of one of the most devastating Native American attacks against the U.S. Army, in which Captain William Fetterman and the 80 men under his command were killed, as shown in a magazine illustration from 1866. The Sioux warrior chief led a successful war against the United States from 1866 to 1868.

while, the Indians negotiated, but on June 13, 1866, another regiment of soldiers arrived at Fort Laramie. Red Cloud was outraged. As Red Cloud left, he said, "Great Father sends us presents and wants new road. But White Chief goes with soldiers to steal road before Indians says yes or no!"

In July of 1866, Red Cloud and his warriors attacked. Throughout the summer of 1866 they continued to skirmish with the soldiers. On December 21, 1866, Red Cloud's warriors, including Crazy Horse, drew the soldiers out of Fort Phil Kearny. Soldiers under the command of Captain William Fetterman pursued them. It was a trap. Indians appeared from either side and killed all 81 of the soldiers. Although the Indians lost more men that day than the Army, "Fetterman's Massacre," as it became known, made a big impression on the U.S. government. It was the worst defeat that Indians had ever inflicted on the U.S. Army to that point.

Red Cloud demanded that the soldiers leave Powder River country or he would not sign a treaty. Finally, the government ordered that the forts

In 1868, General William T. Sherman and other American leaders met at Fort Laramie with Cheyenne and Arapaho Indians to end Red Cloud's War. The resulting treaty yielded the Powder River Valley and the Black Hills to the Native Americans. Americans would violate this treaty within a few years.

in Powder River country be abandoned and that the trail be closed. The troops at Fort C. F. Smith left on July 29, 1868. The next morning a group of warriors led by Red Cloud burned it down. The other forts were abandoned also, and on November 6, 1868, Red Cloud signed the treaty.

In the 1868 Treaty of Fort Laramie, the U.S. government promised that whites would stay out of the Powder River country, and that the Sioux would always possess the Black Hills of South Dakota, which the tribe considered to be a sacred land. For a while, there was peace on the Great Plains. But in the early 1870s, a discovery occurred in the Black Hills that would lead to a new round of frontier warfare.

 TEXT-DEPENDENT QUESTIONS

1. What general led an invasion of the Powder River country in 1865?
2. Which Cheyenne war leader was killed at the Battle of Beecher's Island?
3. Where did "Fetterman's Massacre" occur?

 **RESEARCH PROJECT**

Pick two prominent Native American figures detailed in this chapter and find out how they got their names.

The Medicine Man

Chapter 5

Warfare on the Plains, 1874-1890

When gold was discovered in the Black Hills of South Dakota, the government decided once again to send troops to Sioux territory under the command of George Custer. By the spring of 1875, gold ***prospector***s were swarming the Black Hills. The U.S. Army was supposed to keep the prospectors off Indian land but the soldiers didn't enforce the law. Instead, the U.S. government wanted to buy the land. When Red Cloud wouldn't sell, the U.S. government used the same tactics it had before: they ordered all Native

The frozen body of a Teton Sioux medicine man lies at Wounded Knee Creek, South Dakota. Someone has thrust a rifle into his clenched arms. In truth, almost none of the Sioux were armed when the surprise attack occurred on December 29, 1890. The massacre at Wounded Knee marked the end of the Native American wars on the frontier.

Sitting Bull was considered a formidable fighter, even though he had a pronounced limp, which had been caused by a Crow bullet. He was a member of the Hunkpapa Sioux tribe.

Americans to report to their reservations, while troops hunted down "hostile" Indians.

Though Red Cloud had dealt with the U.S. government in the past, by this time Sitting Bull, a *shaman* known as an excellent planner and organizer, had become a leading chief of the Teton Sioux. The tribe's leading warrior was Crazy Horse.

The Black Hills War of 1876-77, also known as the Great Sioux War, was one of the largest American military undertakings of the late nineteenth century. It was also one of the largest campaigns against Native Americans in U.S. history. Battles were fought in Wyoming, Montana, South Dakota, and Nebraska. The Great Sioux War involved more than 12 armed engagements between the U.S. Army and the Teton Sioux and their allies, the Northern Cheyenne people.

The Great Sioux War was fought for control of approximately 120,000 square miles (310,800 km2) of present-day Nebraska, Wyoming, Montana, as well as North and South Dakota. The Native Americans refused to honor a military ultimatum requiring them to live on an assigned reservation. The white people wanted the Native

 WORDS TO UNDERSTAND IN THIS CHAPTER

melee—a confused struggle.

prospectors—explorers who search for valuable mineral deposits such as gold and silver.

shaman—in Native American culture, a person who uses magic to cure the sick and control events; a "medicine man."

CRAZY HORSE

Crazy Horse, a Teton Sioux warrior, fought to prevent American encroachment on Lakota lands following the Fort Laramie treaty of 1868. He was instrumental in the 1873 attack on a surveying party sent into the Black Hills by General George Custer. Later, Crazy Horse joined forces with Sitting Bull during the counterattack that destroyed Custer's Seventh Cavalry (pictured below). During the winter of 1876–1877, he battled General Nelson Miles as the U.S. Army pursued the Teton Sioux and their allies.

Crazy Horse, a wanted man, had asked his uncle for permission to live with him in peace. His uncle, Spotted Tail, told Crazy Horse that before he could move in with him, he should go to Fort Robinson and explain what he wanted, so he could have the charges against him dropped. Crazy Horse was leery of doing this, because he felt that something terrible would happen. Despite his fear, he followed his uncle's orders.

Apparently, his fear was justified. Before he knew what was happening, Crazy Horse was surrounded by reservation police. He was grabbed and pulled into a prisonlike building, where, later that night, he died.

The death of Crazy Horse is shrouded in mystery. One story goes that, in desperation, Crazy Horse tried to fight his way to freedom with a knife. According to one report, a soldier stabbed Crazy Horse. Another report said that Crazy Horse stabbed himself.

George A. Custer, commander of the Seventh Cavalry, was killed with most of his men at the Battle of the Little Bighorn in June 1876.

Americans' hunting grounds for gold mining.

By May 1876, 45,000 Sioux and their allies were engaged in battle. The U.S. troops were prepared: Horses were shod, tents and baggage packed in wagon trains. Reserve ammunition, hospital supplies, and 10-day rations were transported to the battle site on pack mules. The Native Americans had Winchester repeating rifles, knives, and bows and arrows, while the U.S. troops were armed with carbines and pistols. Each soldier had one blanket and one overcoat. The weather was stormy and rainy in the wide, flat area.

American troops commanded by General George Crook attacked several thousand Sioux camped with Sitting Bull and Crazy Horse at the Rosebud River and were defeated. The Indians then moved their camp to the Little Bighorn River in Montana Territory.

On June 25, 1876, Custer and his troops of the U.S. Seventh Cavalry arrived at the Little Bighorn. Custer thought there was only a small band of Native Americans there; he did not realize that there was an enormous village nearby. The Indians were attacked by Custer from one side and by Major Reno from the other. However, the army quickly was forced to retreat. The Indians killed Custer and all of his men and trapped Reno and his men. When the Indians heard that more troops were coming, they left the area to avoid further fighting.

It was a short-lived victory. The U.S. government decided to punish the innocent Indians who had remained on their reservations. These Indians, who had done nothing, were declared prisoners of war.

Ultimately, the Black Hills War was resolved by treaty. The Teton Sioux ceded the Powder River country and the Black Hills. In return, they received an expansion of their reservation in another direction.

In April of 1877, his warriors starving, Crazy Horse agreed to surrender because the government promised him a reservation in Powder River country. However, Crazy Horse was killed on September 5, 1877.

Sitting Bull would not surrender. In 1877 he fled to Canada. However, he and his people did not stay there long. In July 1881, Sitting Bull returned with his Sioux followers, and they surrendered to American authorities.

The Nez Perce War

Sitting Bull was not the only Native American leader who tried to escape the United States rather than submitting to life on a reservation. In 1855 the Nez Perce tribe had been promised 7.5 million acres of land in Oregon, where they had traditionally lived. However, in 1877, the U.S. government announced plans to move the Nez Perce to a reservation in Idaho.

Chief Joseph of the Nez Perce tried to lead his people to Canada when the settlers drove them from their ancestral land in Oregon. Although they were captured at the border and forced to return to a reservation, the Americans respected his military leadership and dubbed him "the Indian Napoleon."

The Nez Perce leader was Chief Joseph, an eloquent man who was considered a military genius. When the U.S. military was sent to enforce the tribe's move to Idaho, Chief Joseph managed to escape with the tribe. His warriors fought many skirmishes and battles with the American army as they traveled more than 1,700 miles (2,735 km) through Idaho, Wyoming, and Montana. Chief Joseph was trying to reach Canada, where he hoped to join up with Sitting Bull's band of renegade Sioux.

The U.S. Army finally caught up with the Nez Perce in Montana. Around 40 soldiers and 80 native warriors were killed at the Battle of Big Hole in October 1877. The Nez Perce were stopped just 40 miles (64 km) short of the Canadian border. Chief Joseph surrendered and agreed to take his tribe to a reservation in Idaho as the government wanted.

The Ghost Dance and Wounded Knee

In 1888, a Paiute holy man named Wovoka began to tell the Plains Indians that he had received a message from the Creator. He said that in 1891, the world would end and then come back to life. The white men

This magazine illustration from 1877 shows Chief Joseph of the Nez Perce surrendering to General Nelson A. Miles of the U.S. Army. The Nez Perce were trying to leave the United States and settle in Canada, but were stopped by U.S. forces in the Bear Paw Mountains of Montana.

would be destroyed, and the buffalo would once again be plentiful. The dancers would have special shirts that would make them invulnerable to bullets. Soon, a movement began among the Native Americans, with adherents performing chants, meditations, and dances. This movement spread quickly throughout the South and the West. It became known as the Ghost Dance. The Native Americans believed that if they continually practiced the Ghost Dance, the rule of their enemies would end and their freedom would be restored.

Tribes like the Teton Sioux were open to this idea because they sought spiritual guidance. Their lives had been in turmoil because they had been forced to leave their lands and reestablish their lives on reservations.

The Ghost Dance was performed in a circle, with the Native Americans joining hands and slowly shuffling to their left. This dance appeared to raise the hopes of, first, the Sioux, then the Arapaho, Cheyenne, and Kiowa tribes. Although nothing in particular was changing in their lives, performing the dance made them feel less hopeless, as if they were doing something to change the circumstances of their lives.

Wovoka instructed the tribes to perform the dance constantly.

Dancing on Sioux reservations soon became so prevalent that pupils stopped going to school, stores became empty, and little work was accomplished. The white settlers did not understand this whirling, shrieking dance. They were afraid it would inspire Native American uprisings.

In mid-December of 1890, the administrator of the Standing Rock Reservation ordered Sitting Bull to be arrested, because he was afraid that he was going to leave the reservation with the Ghost Dancers. On December 15, 1890, reservation police came to arrest Sitting Bull. Some of the chief's followers tried to prevent the arrest, and Sitting Bull was shot in the *melee*. However, the Native Americans did not retaliate because they believed that, with the Ghost Dance being performed, Sitting Bull would someday come back to life.

After Sitting Bull's death, more than 300 Sioux left the Standing Rock reservation, hoping to join up with Chief Red Cloud at the Pine Ridge reservation in South Dakota. Their leader was Chief Spotted Elk, also known as Big Foot. The U.S. Seventh Cavalry was sent out in pursuit.

In late December, the cavalry caught up with the Sioux at Wounded Knee Creek. They surrounded the Sioux camp and set up four small can-

This drawing of Sioux performing the Ghost Dance was published in 1891. Americans were concerned that the dancers would encourage Native Americans to leave the reservations and go on the warpath.

The Sioux chief Spotted Elk, also known as Big Foot, lies dead in the snow near Wounded Knee Creek. The chief was among the approximately 300 Sioux massacred by the U.S. Seventh Cavalry on December 29, 1890—an attack that marked the end of the Native American wars on the frontier. (Bottom) Dead bodies are strewn around the remains of Spotted Elk's camp

nons. On the morning of December 29, 1890, the soldiers demanded that the Sioux give up their weapons. The Sioux complied, but one warrior did not want to give up his expensive rifle. When a gunshot sounded, the soldiers opened fire. Since the Indians had few weapons, they could not fight back. Around 300 of the Sioux were killed during the massacre that followed. Shootings and stabbings continued throughout the day. Even an interpreter was not safe: Philip Wells was slashed with a long knife, his nose almost torn off. Exploding shells filled the battle area, sparing neither Native American nor U.S. soldier.

The Wounded Knee massacre ended the war on December 29, 1890. A U.S. Army inquest following the massacre concluded that the Native Americans had started the fighting. The official report said that the killing of women and children must have been mostly by Native American bullets; and the Native American attack had been brought on by the Ghost Dance. Colonel James Forsythe, who had been in command at the time of the Wounded Knee battle, was exonerated.

TEXT-DEPENDENT QUESTIONS

1. Why was General George Armstrong Custer considered reckless and rash?
2. What did Crazy Horse's uncle require Crazy Horse to do before he could live with him?

RESEARCH PROJECT

Draw what you think the Sioux and other warriors looked like while Ghost Dancing. Add any details you think might be part of the dance, the area, and the onlookers.

Chronology

1814 On March 27, Andrew Jackson and troops kill 800 Red Stick Creeks at Horseshoe Bend in Alabama. In August, the Creeks sign a treaty giving up 23 million acres of land in Georgia and Alabama.

1824 The Bureau of Indian Affairs is created as part of the War Department.

1830 President Andrew Jackson signs the Indian Removal Act into law on May 28.

1838 Cherokees begin a forced relocation to Indian Territory; thousands die on the "Trail of Tears."

1845 James K. Polk is elected president. Expansion into Indian territories will be encouraged.

1848 The United States wins the war against Mexico, acquiring a significant amount of territory in the southwest. Gold is discovered in California, drawing thousands of new settlers to the West.

1861 The Navajo War begins in Arizona and New Mexico.

1862 Congress passes the Homestead Act, which allows citizens to settle on up to 160 acres of unclaimed public land in the western territories and receive title to it after living there for five years. In Minnesota, angry Sioux attempt to drive white settlers from the region. The uprising results in the execution of 39 Sioux ringleaders, while more than 1,600 others are sent to a reservation in South Dakota.

1863 The Apache chief Mangas Coloradas is killed by whites who had lured him to what he thought was a peace parley.

1864 Kit Carson and General James Carleton end Navaho resistance, forcing the Navaho to live on the reservation at Bosque

Redondo; on November 29, members of the Cheyenne tribe are massacred at Sand Creek.

1865 General Patrick Connor leads an expedition into the Powder River country, but fails to stop Native American attacks on settlers traveling the Bozeman Trail.

1866 In December, U.S. forces suffer a significant defeat when 80 men are killed in the "Fetterman Massacre" near Fort Phil Kearney.

1867 Congress forms the "Peace Commission" to convince Great Plains Indians to move to reservations. Many tribes resist.

1868 Red Cloud drives U.S. troops out of Powder River country; on November 26, Custer's Seventh Calvary slaughters Black Kettle and many women and children near Fort Cobb, Oklahoma.

1869 Fort Sill is built in Oklahoma as a base for the military aggression against Native Americans in the Indian Territory.

1873 The Model 1873 lever action rifle is introduced by Winchester Firearms. No rifle came to symbolize the romance of the West more than this gun.

1874 Gold is discovered in the Black Hills of South Dakota, leading to a rush of prospectors in this land. The region, considered sacred by the Sioux, had been promised to them in the 1868 Treaty of Fort Laramie; the arrival of whites increased tensions among the Native Americans.

1876 On June 17, a large force under General George Crook is forced to break off its pursuit of the Sioux after a defeat at the Battle of the Rosebud. Custer's defeat at the Little Bighorn River on June 25 is a major defeat for the U.S. Army in the West.

1877 American troops hunt down Great Plains Indians and force them onto reservations. Americans try to impose white culture on Indians. Sitting Bull escapes to Canada with about 300 followers. Crazy Horse surrenders and is killed at Fort Robinson, Nebraska. After leading the Nez Perce on a running fight for more than 1,000 miles, Chief Joseph is surrounded by American troops and surrenders just 40 miles from the Canadian border.

1886   Geronimo surrenders, ending the Apache Wars.

1887   Congress passes the Dawes Act, which allots land to individual Indians rather than to tribes as a whole. The project is a disaster for Indians.

1890   The Wounded Knee Massacre on December 29 brings an end to Native American resistance.

Further Reading

Collins, Charles D. Jr. *Atlas of the Sioux Wars*, 2nd ed. Fort Leavenworth, KS: Combat Studies Institute Press, 2006.

DiSilvestro, Roger L. *In the Shadow of Wounded Knee*. New York: Walker & Company, 2007.

Drury, Bob. *The Heart of Everything That Is: The Untold Story of Red Cloud, An American Legend*. New York: Simon & Schuster, 2013.

Gwynne, S.C. *Empire of the Summer Moon: Quanah Parker and the Rise and Fall of the Comanches, the Most Powerful Indian Tribe in American History*. New York: Scribner, 2010.

Kessel, William B., and Robert Wooster. *Encyclopedia Of Native American Wars And Warfare*. New York: Facts on File, 2005.

Marshall, Joseph M. *The Journey of Crazy Horse: A Lakota History*. New York: Viking, 2004.

Osborn, William M. *The Wild Frontier*. New York: Random House, 2000.

Philbrick, Nathaniel. *The Last Stand: Custer, Sitting Bull, and the Battle of the Little Bighorn*. New York: Penguin, 2010.

Powers, Thomas. *The Killing of Crazy Horse*. New York: Random House, 2010.

Utley, Robert M. *The Frontier Regulars: The United States Army and the Indians, 1866–1890*. New York: Macmillan Publishing Co., 1974.

Utley, Robert M., and Wilcomb E. Washburn. *The American Heritage History of the Indian Wars*. New York: American Heritage Publishing Co., 1977.

Internet Resources

http://www.fpri.org/docs/media/skarsted.pdf
This essay by Vance Skarstedt provides an in-depth analysis of the causes of Native American wars on the frontier during the nineteenth century.

http://www.amhistory.si.edu/militaryhistory/exhibition/
This website features facts about Geronimo and Native American reservations, with good photographs.

http://prezi.com/qnaa6qsygxrk/indianwars
Includes a basic outline of the Native American frontier wars, plus a concise time line of battles.

Index

Alabama, 11
American buffalo (bison), *7*, 14, 16, *17*
Anthony, Scott J., 38
Apache, 27-33
Arapaho, 16, 17, 21, *35*, 40, 41, 42, 52
Arihara, 16
Arizona, 8
Arkansas, 12
Assiniboine, 16

Battle of Beecher's Island, *43*
Battle of Big Hole, 51
Battle of Horseshoe Bend, 11
Battle of the Little Bighorn, 50
Battle of Punished Woman Fork, 20-22
Battle of the Rosebud, 50
Big Foot. *See* Spotted Elk
bison. *See* American buffalo
Black Hills, 9, 46, 47, 50
Black Hills War (Great Sioux War), 48-51
Black Kettle, 38, 39
Bosque Redondo, 29
Bozeman Trail, 41, 42

California, 8, 9, *21*, 22, 23
Canada, 51
Canby, Edward, 23
Carleton, James, 28, 29
Carson, Kit, *29*
Cherokee, 11, 12
Cheyenne, 16, 21, *35*, 40, 41, 42, 43, 52
Chicasaw, *12*
Chivington, John M., *38*, 39, 40
Choctaw, *12*, 13
Cochise, 28, 29, 33
Colorado, 8, 7, 38, 39, 40, 43
Comanche, 30
Connor, Patrick E., 41,
Crazy Horse, 33, 45, 48, *49*, 50
Creek, 11, *12*
Crook, George, 34, 50

Crow, 17
Custer, George A., 47, *49*, 50

Delaware, 10
Dull Knife, 21

Fetterman, William, *44*, 45
Florida, 8, 34
Forsythe, James, 55
Fort Cobb, 39
Fort Defiance, 28
Fort Phil Kearny, 45
Fort Laramie, *15*, 45

Georgia, 11, 12
Geronimo, *32*, 33-34
Ghost Dance movement, 51-55
Great Lakes, 10
Great Sioux War. *See* Black Hills War
Gros Ventre, 16

Hancock, Winfield Scott, 42

Idaho, 51
Illinois, 10, 12
Indian Territory, *9*, 12, 13
Indian Removal Act, 11
Indiana, 10, 11

Jackson, Andrew, 11, 12
Chief Joseph, 33, 51

Kansas, 8, 17, 21, 43
Kintpuash (Captain Jack), 22, 23, 24
Kiowa, 52
Klamath, 22, 23

Lakota. *See* Teton Sioux.
Lewis, William H., 21
Little Crow, 36, 37
Little Turtle, 10

Numbers in ***bold italics*** refer to captions.

Little Wolf, 21
Louisiana Purchase, 8

Mandan, 16
Mangas Coloradas, 27, 28
Manuelito, 28, *29*, 30
Mexican War, 8, *9*, 27
Michigan, 10
Miles, Nelson A., *33*, 34Modoc, 22, 23, 24
Minnesota, 35, 36, 37
Missouri, 12, 13
Modoc War, 22, 23
Montana, 17, 51

Navajo, 28, 29
Nebraska, *16*, 17
Nevada, 8
New Mexico, 8, 17, 43
New Ulm, *36*, 37
Nez Perce, 51
North Dakota, 17, 35
Northwest Ordinance (1787), 10

Ohio, 10, 11
Ojibway, 10
Oklahoma, 8, 13, 17, 21, 43.
    See also Indian Territory
Oregon, 51,
Oregon Trail, 14
Ottawa, 10

Paiute, 51
Pawnee, 17
Pine Ridge Reservation, *25*
Polk, James K., 8
Potawatomi, 10
Powder River country, 40-42, 50

Quanah Parker, *30*

Ramsey, Alexander, 37
Red Cloud, *44*, 45, 46, 47, 48, 53
Red Cloud's War, 44-46
Red River War, 30-31, 33
Roman Nose, *41*, 42-43

San Carlos Reservation, 33
Sand Creek massacre, *35*, 38-40

Santee Sioux, 35, *36*, 37, 38
Seminole, *12*
Sitting Bull, *48*, 50, 51, 53
Shawnee, 10
Sheridan, Philip, 43
Shoshone, 40
Sibley, Henry, 37
South Dakota, 9, 17, 35, 46
Spain, 8
Spotted Elk (Big Foot), 53, *54*
Standing Rock Reservation, 53
Sutter's Mill, 15

Texas, 8, 17, 28, 33, 43
Teton Sioux, 16, *22*, 25, 35, 37, 40, 41, 48,
    50, 52, 53-55
Trail of Tears, *12*
Transcontinental Railroad, 9
Treaty of Fort Laramie (1851), 15-16
Treaty of Fort Laramie (1868), 46, 49
Treaty of Greenville, 10

Unorganized Territory. *See* Indian
    Territory
Utah, 8

Victorio's War, 31-32
Victorio, *31*, 32

Worcester v. Georgia (1832), 12
Wounded Knee massacre, 53-55
Wovoka, 51, 52
Wyoming, 8, 17, 51

 # SERIES GLOSSARY

blockade—an effort to cut off supplies, war material, or communications by a particular area, by force or the threat of force.

guerrilla warfare—a type of warfare in which a small group of combatants, such as armed civilians, use hit-and-run tactics to fight a larger and less mobile traditional army. The purpose is to weaken an enemy's strength through small skirmishes, rather than fighting pitched battles where the guerrillas would be at a disadvantage.

intelligence—the analysis of information collected from various sources in order to provide guidance and direction to military commanders.

logistics—the planning and execution of movements by military forces, and the supply of those forces.

salient—a pocket or bulge in a fortified line or battle line that projects into enemy territory.

siege—a military blockade of a city or fortress, with the intent of conquering it at a later stage.

tactics—the science and art of organizing a military force, and the techniques for using military units and their weapons to defeat an enemy in battle.